WHAT IS MY PURPOSE?

WHAT IS MY PURPOSE?

By

Charles Thomas Jr.

ISBN: 978-0-7596-0897-9 (sc)
ISBN: 978-0-7596-0896-2 (e)

This book is printed on acid-free paper.

1stBooks - rev. 1/19/01

INTRODUCTION

I was born the fourth of ten children to Charles and Bernice Thomas in Cincinnati, Ohio, where I spent the first twelve years of my life.

We were a very poor family, but with the help of God, extended family, and close friends, we were able to get beyond the things we did not have. It was a life that seemed simple (a perception that probably had something to do with my age), but the inability to make ends meet caused things to become more complicated quickly.

When I was about ten-years-old, my father moved to Detroit, Michigan, to seek suitable employment. He left my mother with what was then nine children. . She was up to the task and kept us in line and together. In spite of this and the support of those around us, it could not save us from being victimized when it became evident that we were left basically unprotected.

Our home was broken into on several occasions, two of which I remember very vividly even today. One time, when we left home to go to the drive-in, we returned to intruders in our house. We lived in a row house then, and instead of running away, one thief stood in the shadows at the edge of the row house watching us outside, while the others inside took what they wanted and left.

They weren't afraid of my mother and us children -- the oldest being my 13-year-old sister.

On another occasion, we were at home late at night and asleep. A would-be burglar tried coming in through the window, but my mother's outraged shouting turned him away.

Such intrusions became too common, and I was relieved when I received the news that my father was returning to move the family to a home he had purchased for us in Michigan.

We moved and left behind everything that I had ever known -- home.... friends.... family -- but of all the things I thought I might miss, I never imagined how much I would miss the comfort that came with being in the same school system. Up until then, I was able to walk into a classroom, afraid though I was, and still see all my friends. This made it a little easier to handle transitions into each new school year, but the move to Detroit proved to be quite traumatic.

When I went into the Detroit Public School system, I wanted to fit in, but I had two things going against me. Not only was I new, I had also broken my leg playing football my last summer in Ohio, so instead of being able to blend in, I stuck out like a sore thumb.

In the Cincinnati school system, I had been a straight "A" student, and in Detroit, I continued to achieve some of the highest scores on state tests for Michigan. Even with this good academic standing, it didn't help me because I was being exposed to things that I had never been exposed to before in my life. It was a time when gang violence was on the rise, and survival became more important than being educated.

At home, things were getting worse. The move that was supposed to bring our family together seemed to cause it to grow further apart. Even though my father had acquired a job with one of the big three automakers, my parents continually argued over money and the need to improve our living conditions by giving more attention to housecleaning. Their arguments were often heated and grew to the point where they became violent. I was sensitive enough to the situation to realize that it was either going to cause someone to be seriously injured or lead to divorce.

Things came to a head for me at the age of 15. My visits to the classroom became more and more infrequent. In all honesty, I was not only afraid for my well being, I also couldn't see how learning geometry was going to help me subsidize my parents' income to fix the situation at home.

At the age of 16 I went from being one of the best students in the system to a drop out attending night school. This allowed me to take on the task of cleaning the entire household. From top to bottom, seven days a week, I cleaned a house that was occupied by my parents and nine siblings.

This took care of one of my problems, but there was still no money.

At the age of 17, moving toward the 11th grade but at the same time going nowhere, I made a life-changing decision. I decided to take the test to join the Armed Forces. This meant that I also had to be satisfied with a G.E.D. (General Equivalency Diploma) I took the test and passed easily.

During my five-and-a-half-year military tour, I sent most of my income home. I thought this would be the answer to what I had taken on as my problem, but it did not prevent my parents' inevitable divorce seven years later.

In the mean time, I was a boy trying to make it in a man's world. The week that I left home to begin my military service, I drank my first half can of beer. A few months after my 17th birthday, I was shipped to Germany. Germany was a different world. Drugs, alcohol, and promiscuous living were the order of the day. I found myself in places and involved in things that I could never have imagined.

Through all of my experience, with all that I lost and gave up, I found that it did not have to be the end of my story. I was able to gain some College experience and, because of my work ethic, make a good living. I now have a very beautiful wife and two very beautiful children.

More importantly, I discovered that I could still be connected to the purpose for which I was originally created. Though What Is My Purpose is not my autobiography, it is my story in the sense that I found out that, with God, I could still find the peace that goes along with living life within the context of my purpose.

This book is my attempt, through the urgings of the Holy Spirit, to help others discover "What Is My Purpose?"

CHAPTER ONE

RETURNING TO THE GARDEN

One of the greatest mysteries that man has to unfold along his life's journey is the mystery of discovering his purpose.

We are given a task at birth of fulfilling a destiny that was given to us even before we were conceived.

Being creations of destiny we are born with an appetite for accomplishment and fulfillment.

The problem with this is the sad and sometimes tragic reality that there are people who live and die having never discovered the reason why they were created in the first place.

There are those who even get as far as discovering our purpose, and even with this knowledge, never complete the task that has been assigned to us.

Whichever state we may find ourselves in, we still have to contend with the fact that this appetite exists within us that needs to be attended to.

If this appetite is to be satisfied, we must first establish a beginning, or starting point in our quest to find out who it is we are destined to be.

However, it is my contention that, if we are to discover who we are, we first have to discover what we are.

So, in our quest to discover who we are and what we are meant to become, the best place to start is with our beginnings. To do this, we must take a trip back to the Garden.

In the biblical account in Genesis, we see God creating a Utopian environment for man.

God created the Heavens and the earth, the night and day, the herbs and fruit, the fish and the fowl, the cattle and the beasts of the earth with man's needs and pleasure in mind.

After He finished creating everything man needed, God created man "in His image and after His own likeness."

Along with those qualities of image and likeness came intrinsic attributes that, in and of themselves, cannot be defined as our purpose, but these attributes need to be discovered, explored and developed if we are ever to discover and fulfill what our purpose really is.

As part of this package of image and likeness, God inherently gives to us attributes that include things like desire, reason, emotion and choice.

These qualities in and of themselves are good, but God being God knew the problems that man could and would create for himself with the misuse of these attributes. In spite of this, man was given these liberties, and they were all part of the package when God breathed into the nostrils of what he formed from the dust of the earth and allowed for man to become a living soul.

When we look further into the story, we see that it did not take Adam long to find the trouble that went along with the improper exercise of these attributes. But before we get too far into our history, we see that not only did God give Adam these intrinsic attributes, He also gave him extrinsic employment so that man would not be left to live out his existence without a purpose.

According to Genesis 1:28 God employed Adam when he told him to "be fruitful and multiply." God told Adam to "fill the earth and subdue it" and to "have dominion over every living thing." In the 15th verse of the second chapter, God instructed Adam to tend to the garden that He placed him in.

When we look to the garden, we have to understand that, just as God did for Adam, He also did for us. God gave us a place of employment and a destiny to fulfill. We need to go through the process of discovery, but when we go through this process of discovery, there is something that we need to take into account that was not an issue when Adam was initially given his assignment.

In my estimation, this issue is even more significant than any of the technological advances that God used man to invent to change our world for the good, and advance mankind to the degree that we see today.

When it comes to our purpose, we need to take into account that when sin made its entrance into the equation that it not only changed Adam's purpose individually, but it also changed and is changing the individual purposes of man collectively.

These changes that sin brought about, though incomparable to anything when it comes to its effect on our world, are nevertheless no cause for great concern if we recognize that in spite of the fact that God is immutable, He still works in space and time.

Part of the changing face of the world through the progression of time is the decimation, disarray and destruction that is all around us, and we have to understand that it is all a product of sin.

These visible effects of sin differ geographically, but it does not change the fact that the effects are still prevalent wherever we are.

This problem of sin is the primary cause for all the negative effects of change in our world, and just as things changed for Adam, sin is cause for continual change for us.

Included in these changes are the inception of and the continual intrusion of sin.

These changes brought about by sin call for differing gifts and administrations to those gifts.

Based upon this fact, we can see how a Pastor in an affluent community in the United States and a Missionary in an impoverished city in Haiti would have different purposes.

I know that you would say that their purposes are the same, and ultimately that would be true, which would be to introduce those that they minister to our Savior.

Yes, I agree that ultimately their purposes would be the same, but the way God would employ them in service would be different.

Herein lies my point. When we look at this Pastor and this Missionary, we have to understand that even though their purposes are similar, sin has caused the way that they will be employed to carry them out to differ. In spite of the differences, they will only be able to arrive at a conclusion the same way.

What I'm trying to say is that just as it was with Adam and Eve, it will be with us.

When God created man, and everything that man ever would need, He also included the ability to either carry out His purpose and the choice (for lack of a better way to put it) to mess everything up.

Therefore, in order to discover our purpose, we must first recognize that when God originally created us in the person of Adam, He made us with desires and emotions, and the ability to reason and choose.

This is ultimately important because just as the improper exercise of choice caused Adam's plan and purpose to be altered from what God originally planned, it is the same for us.

When that Pastor and that Missionary look to fulfill their purpose, they must do it by first realizing that they and the people that they minister to have the qualities that come along with being created in the image of God, and that the improper exercise of these attributes causes their purpose to continually change.

What I am suggesting is that the more we allow our desires and emotions to draw us away from God, and the more our reason and choices are out of line with the will of God, the further we will find ourselves from the image of God.

As we drift along through life in this condition of allowing ourselves to be led further away from

His image, it drives us further away from our purpose.

This is why we must return to the garden. The garden gives us a picture of all that man was initially created with, and a reference for the process to be used to determine who God created us to be.

Adam's sin caused him to fall from the image of God, and God drove Adam from the Utopia that was the garden, and along with it he was driven from the place where he was to fulfill his destiny.

So, if we are to become people of destiny who know what we are created to be, we must first recognize who we are.

When it comes to discovering who we really are, sin has increased the degree of difficulty. It has caused us to be born with vision that is blurred from the womb, and without the original idea we have no frame of reference.

Therefore, if we are to know who it is that we are created to be, we must first recognize who we are.

So, it is imperative that we return to the garden.

CHAPTER TWO

RESTORING THE IMAGE

As we have discussed in Chapter One, it is imperative to understand that we first recognize who we are.

In our trip to the Garden, we discovered that we are created in the image and likeness of God.

As part of the package that goes along with His image, God has given us some intrinsic qualities and/or attributes that were damaged when Adam fell. These intrinsic qualities were given to Adam as the governing authority when he carried out the duties of his extrinsic purpose. In other words, what was inside of Adam was supposed to dictate to him how he was to carry out the purpose that God created him to fulfill.

When Adam went about the process of fulfilling these responsibilities that God placed in his hands, he was supposed to be motivated and moved by urgings of a purity that was a product of an unblemished image.

When Adam sinned, he placed a stain on the image that he was originally created with, and that sin separated him from God, caused him to be sidetracked from his purpose and to abandon his post.

The problem that now exists is a genetic problem because the sin that entered into Adam's bloodstream has been passed down to us all. It is this that caused the Psalmist to cry out in his confession, "Behold I was shapen in iniquity and in sin did my mother conceive me."

Given that we are all born in this condition, we start out on a road that is not in line with our extrinsic purpose, because we are not aligned with our intrinsic purpose.

This separation that has damaged our original image through Adam, and has caused us to be out of alignment with God, has also caused us to be out of alignment with our purpose.

What I am trying to say is that, if our problem with discovering our extrinsic purpose is due to damage that has been done to us intrinsically, before we can fully discover our purpose, we must first repair the damage done internally by rediscovering His image.

Therefore, if we are to move from this point, we need to go through the process of restoring the damage that has been done to our image.

When we look at Adam, we see a man who was placed in a Utopian environment in the Garden.

Adam was given everything that he needed, not only to exist but also to live a life as close to Heaven as could ever be provided on earth.

With that, Adam was given access to everything in the Garden with the exception of one thing. Adam was instructed by God in Genesis 2: 16 & 17: "Of every tree of the garden you may freely eat; but of the tree of the knowledge of good and evil, you shall not eat, for in the day you eat of it, you shall surely die."

In as much as I know how familiar the record of this event was, it goes without saying that Adam failed to follow His instructions, but what we need to see is that, when Adam partook of the tree, it placed an indelible mark not only on Adam's soul but also on the soul of all that would come after him.

For the sake of explanation, it should be clearly understood that, when I say indelible, I am in no way suggesting that the power of God, and the sacrifice made by our Savior, is insufficient for the blotting out of our sins.

The sacrifice that Christ made was not only sufficient for access in to Heaven after I die, but according to 1st John 3:2 it causes God to see us as everything that we are going to be in spite of the fact we are in the condition we are in.

What I am suggesting is that, when Adam sinned, he fathered a predicament in life that can only be fully satisfied for man after death.

When Adam sinned, all of humankind fell with him. Sin contaminated his bloodstream and caused him to be driven by an appetite that had distaste for the things of God.

Adam's transgression caused his eyes to be opened, and he began to see things from a perspective that God did not intend for man to see.

With the inception of sin came a self-conscious, self-serving, self-gratifying drive that pulled Adam away from his originally created purpose.

These drives were passed down through Adam's blood and caused all of humankind to be born with the natural proclivity to sin. It is that drive that caused Paul in the 7th chapter of the book of Romans to cry out with the voice of what most consider to be the saved, "What I will to do, I do not, and what I hate, that I do."

Paul's only consolation was that it was no longer him, but the sin that dwelt in him.

In spite of that, we still have a war that we must fight daily, whether saved or unsaved, that without the power of God dominates our lives.

Again keep in mind that I have taken us down this road because there is a point that we need to arrive at. That is: we have to establish the fact that if we are going to discover what our purpose is, we must first re-discover His.

In the 60s, this process of discovery was defined by the statement: "I need to go and find myself." That phrase is the best way to describe the point I am driving toward, but the sad truth is that the majority of the people that made that statement spent their lifetime looking and never arrived at their destined purpose because they were trying to find something, not really understanding that what was lost was them.

What they failed to understand is that they could never come to a conclusion as to what they were until they first established who God wanted them to be.

We can see historically, as well as biblically, that when it was the desire of men to move a people away from what they were destined to be, they sought to take away their identity.

We see that in our own American history, as well as in the biblical history of the Jews.

When the Babylonians forced slavery upon the nation of Israel, they moved them out of their cities, they enforced a new lifestyle, and they changed their names in an attempt to totally separate them from their identity.

As if that was not enough, to punctuate all that they inflicted upon the children of Israel, the Babylonians burned down their cities so that the last thing that the Israelites would see as they were carried off into captivity was that there was nothing to ever return to.

In spite of the fact that we know that this was allowed by God to carry out His judgment on the nation of Israel, the truth of the matter still remains. That truth is that the idea was to take away everything that they could use to identify who they were as a people and reprogram them with the idea of who they (the Babylonians) wanted them to be.

The Babylonians sought to take away everything that Israel knew physically, emotionally and spiritually.

This is what the Devil does to us with sin.

He enslaved us by making us the servants of sin. He separated us from our nation. He altered our lifestyle. In short, he robbed us of our identity.

Therefore, if we are truly going to discover our purpose, we must first rediscover God's. If we are to find ourselves, we have to see ourselves through the eyes of the One who created us.

We need to discover God's purpose.

The good thing about this quest is that we don't have to leave home to find it. God has left us with the manual that will tell us what His purpose is.

There are two amusing things that you will find when we look at the answer to the question of what God's purpose is:

1. The answer is found in one of the most familiar and often quoted passages in the bible.

If I were to ask anyone that has been on this Christian journey for a time to turn to Romans 8:28 in their Bible--without opening their Bible--they would probably quote from memory: "And we know that all things work together for good to them that love God, to them that are called according to His purpose."

Few of that number who could quote verse 28 would know what it says in verse 29, but it is in that 29th verse that we can find what God's purpose for our lives is. As obvious as this should be based upon what is stated in verse 28, this is not the second of the two things that I find so amusing. The second thing is:

2. His purpose now is no different than the purpose that He originally created us with.

Romans 8:29 tells us that God's purpose is to restore to us what Adam lost for us in the garden. That 29th verse begins by making the statement:

"For whom He did foreknow, He also did predestinate to be conformed to the image of His Son..."

Just as He did with Adam, God has an extrinsic purpose for our lives, but in order to fulfill it, He wants to give back to us what we had intrinsically. God wants to conform us back to His image.

It needs to be stated for the sake of clarity that this restoration does not free us from the problems that come along with our fallen nature. Just as Paul stated in the 7th chapter of Romans, we still have a war that takes place in our members, so when we look to God for restoration through the person of Jesus Christ, we have to understand that, in spite of the fact that salvation is right now, restoration is a process. The problem now is that our nature has to be conformed to what was supposed to come naturally.

This need for restoration is not simply a matter of what we inherited from Adam.

Our original image is not only damaged by nature, it has also been damaged through nurture.

In life we have come in contact with those who have driven us further away from what God intended for us to become.

These acts, whether intentional or unintentional, can cause us to become callused and more entrenched in a life of sin and self-destruction. It has caused it to become more difficult for us to find the path that leads us back to God, and to stay on it once we find it.

This struggle to be conformed back to God's image lives with us daily, but the good news is He does not leave us to do what is now unnatural, with the expectation that we will accomplish it on our own.

In spite of the fact that man's distorted reasoning and desires were a product of his own sin, God did not leave man alone, to do what is no longer natural, subject to his own nature. God through Jesus Christ gave us a Gift that is supernatural that gives us the power to conform.

So, if we are going to be successful in fulfilling our extrinsic purpose, we have to first discover our intrinsic purpose.

We need to allow God to give us back what we lost in the garden.

We have to allow him to give us the power to be conformed to the process of restoring our image.

CHAPTER THREE

THE CREATION PACKAGE

TALENTS AND GIFTS

As we have discussed in the earlier chapters, God has given us an intrinsic as well as extrinsic purpose. This purpose, though beneficial to us, is not exclusive to just what make our lives better.

With this in mind, we need to understand that, just as it was with Adam, it is also with us that God has given us a purpose that He expects us to fulfill.

Now that we have made our trek through the garden and discovered who we are, and have committed to the process of allowing God to restore to us what was lost with our fallen image, we need to look at the steps we need to take in order to discover our extrinsic purpose.

When we look at Adam and what God prescribed for him as his purpose, we see how God operated within the economy of Adam's existence.

After God ended the work that He had done in creating the Heavens and the earth, he charged Adam with the responsibility of maintaining dominion over His creation. God told Adam to subdue the earth and to fill it, to be fruitful and multiply.

This individual purpose for Adam was given to him based upon his time and place, as well as the abilities that God placed in him.

Adam, being the beginning of human creation, was given the responsibility of procreation and maintaining the garden that God placed him in.

In other words, it was within the economy of his existence.

At this point, I think it is important that we understand two things.

We must first recognize that:

1. When it comes to ability or talents, all men are not created equal.

Now for some of us who are not yet mature, this will be the cause for feelings of jealousy and envy.

If we are in the group that finds themselves in this company, and remain immature, these feelings will eventually lead to animosity and bitterness. (Not that we would want to trace these feelings back to its source; we will just leave it said that the distributing of these talents are in the hand of God.) If these feelings go unchecked, we will find ourselves becoming critical, disenchanted and eventually separated from the body of Christ.

As a word of consolation, it needs to be stated that feelings of this nature are not uncommon.

We can be comfortable with the community that God places us in one day and the next day find ourselves totally dissatisfied, but if we are to win this war, we will win it with a maturity that comes from a battle that has to be fought within us, through the power of the Spirit of God.

For others of us who have come to a more mature place in God, this will be the source of great relief.

When we come to terms with the fact that God divides talents or gifts "severally as He wills" (1 Cor. 12:18), we free ourselves to live out our purpose in God, and not get lost in what seems to be the glory we perceive that can be received in someone else's.

Secondly, we need to come to terms with the fact that:

2. Every charge is not our charge.

Just as I stated earlier, God's purpose for our lives is founded in the economy in which God creates us. It includes elements such as time and place, but a common mistake is the exclusion of the ability that God places in us.

Just for the sake of clarity it must be stated that by no means am I suggesting that God is limited by any of these.

When it comes to time, place, and abilities, God works within them, but is not limited by any of them.

One of the more frequently occurring examples of this we can see in the life of Abraham.

God gave Abraham abilities to fulfill his purpose for a particular time, but in order to accomplish His purpose, God had to move him to a different place.

On rare occasions, when the time and place were in line with what God seeks to accomplish through man, God gives more ability. This we can see in the life of Elisha when he was called to follow in the footsteps of Elijah. In order to be able to do what God would have him do, he was given what the Bible describes as a double portion.

On even more rare occasions, God has even granted man more time. Just as he did for Joshua when the Israelites were engaged in battle with the Amorites.

The Israelites found themselves in the midst of a battle that Joshua determined they were not going to be able to complete because there was not enough time left in the day. According to the book of Joshua in the 10th chapter, 12th -14th verses,

Joshua spoke to the Lord, and He caused the sun to stand still for about a whole day.

This issue of how God is not limited by time is not just limited to one day.

The book of II Kings records King Hezekiah earnestly praying to God and God granting him 15 more years. (Though most believe this was not in the perfect will of God.)

So we have to understand that when we seek out our purpose in God that, even though He works in time and space, He is by no means subject to any of them.

God has power to go beyond all of our faults and failures. He is not limited by our history or inadequacies.

With God nothing is impossible, and because it's not impossible for Him, it's always possible for us.

Those things that we are not able to do--if God wants us to do them--He will give us more ability to do them.

If we are not in the place where God would have us to be, God will either move us to that place, or He will change the place to put us in position, so that His will can be done.

All that aside, we still have to recognize that God has some specific things that he wants to accomplish through us and that just because there is an open door does not mean that it is our door.

God bears no expectation that a member of the body that is gifted to be an usher fail attempting to be the teacher for the vacant teen Sunday school class. He no more expects that of the usher than He expected Peter to go into the lion's den.

We have to understand that we might be in the right place at the right time, with a door of service open to us, but that door may not be the door that God has ordained for us. There are specific areas of service that are in line with God's will for us.

I don't believe that there is any more painful experience in the church of God than watching someone that is gifted to be an usher, dying (and killing others in the process) while attempting to teach a class in Sunday school.

It does not take long to discover that is not their gift.

If we are ever going to clear up this confusion, and function with the cohesion in which a body is supposed to function, we need to answer the question that Paul asked when he was converted on the road to Damascus.

When Paul came to the realization that he was operating outside of the will of God, and wrestling against the power of God, in an act of ultimate surrender he asked the question: "Lord, what will thou have me to do?"

This is what I call the question of purpose.

When we ask this question sincerely we move from the position of what would be self-gratifying to the position of allowing God to use us in what will be fulfilling.

This question of purpose is one that can be easily answered if we begin to ask the right question.

At the risk of being overly simple, I believe that we can find the answers when we seek to find out who God made us to be and stop focusing on what God made somebody else to be.

What we need to do is unwrap the gifts that were given to us as part of the creation package.

Not that we are limited to these. Faithfulness over a few things makes room for many, but there are gifts that all of us are created with and we need to discover those gifts.

This is an argument that is not only supported biblically but also naturally.

In our world, we can find unsaved administrators that are equally as gifted as administrators who are saved.

If we search hard enough, we can find we can find unsaved teachers that teach just as well as ones who are saved.

We can also find speakers who speak just as well as those who speak from a pulpit on any given Sunday, and dare I say that some of those that are extremely dynamic speaking from those pulpits are unsaved.

In the 7th chapter of Matthew, Jesus speaks of the many who would come to Him and claim to have done many wonders in His name who will be turned away because, in a way that a Father knows His own children, Jesus says that He never knew them.

The point is that whether they are spiritual or fleshly, saved or unsaved, believer or unbeliever, they are all gifted with abilities that were a part of the creation package.

Those gifts may be the same or they may differ, and even if they are the same they are administered differently.

The point is that whatever those gifts are, they are a part of the creation package.

This is why we cannot limit Acts 17: 28 to the fact that we are animated. Animals have life and the ability to be mobile, but they do not have being in the sense that humans have being.

Most of what animals are able to accomplish is based on instinct, drive and motor skills.

They can also be taught through training to perform with the use of stimuli, but they are, for the most part, just equipped with what it takes to survive.

Humans, on the other hand, are not limited to what comes instinctively. We are created with God-given talents and gifts. These gifts are given to be increased upon and go far beyond what is needed for our basic survival.

They give us the capacity to lend to, develop, and add to society as we know it, and it is all a part of the creation package.

To ignore this, we give credence to theories espoused by men like Darwin, Hitler and Jim Crow.

It perpetuates the idea of superiority and allows men to feel justified with the notion of the need for segregation, extermination and ultimately the extinction of those who are inferior to them.

In creation, we see how the fowl of the air, the fish in the sea, the cattle, the beast and every creeping thing--even the vegetation--were created with life, but only man was breathed into with the breath of God to become a human being.

When God breathed into the nostrils of man, that breath did not just consist of nitrogen and oxygen. Along with it came an intelligence that defines who we are created to be.

This intelligence is not something that has to be attained or sought after. We possess it.

It defines what we are created to be.

It is part of the creation package.

So, we look to the Garden to discover who we are, and we look at ourselves through the process of self-discovery to find out what we are created to be, understanding that, whatever it is, it's all a part of the package.

CHAPTER FOUR

RESPONDING TO THE REVELATION

Now that we have dealt with the process of discovering the purposes and abilities that God has borne in us, what we need to do now is learn how to properly respond to what we have discovered through the process of revelation.

This would seem like the easiest part of the process, because once God reveals to us what He would have us do, the proper response would be just to do it.

As easy as it sounds, it is sad to say that this is where most of us fail.

There are a couple of reasons that come to mind as to why this might be happening, so instead of looking at the proper response to what is being revealed (which is very obviously to just say, "Yes") we will look at the things that keep us from instantly responding properly.

The first thing that causes us to respond improperly is that we don't recognize that there is more than one thing being revealed.

We have already discussed it in our earlier chapters, but it bears repeating again that there is an intrinsic and extrinsic purpose for man.

We find ourselves confused because we miss the fact that initially we are being called to the need to have our fallen image restored.

This is the first and foremost revelation from God.

Without the proper response to this revelation, we cannot properly respond to, nor totally fulfill the second revelation.

The second of the two problems is as I just stated: trying to be successful extrinsically, bypassing what is necessary intrinsically.

Again, I feel it must be stated that, not only do I believe that it is possible for the unsaved to discover their gift(s), but I also believe that they can be very successful in the exercise of them.

As I stated earlier, there are administrators, teachers, speakers and those that are gifted in many other fields that are just as extraordinary in their fields as their saved counterparts.

The issue is that, even though they may be extraordinary in their external exercise of their gifts, they cannot totally fulfill what they are purposed to do. The reason for this is that being externally successful is not the ultimate goal for creation.

God desires for us to embrace the fact that success cannot be summed up simply in what we accomplish in time.

If we are to arrive at a state of ultimate success when it comes to fulfilling our purpose, we have to understand that the external purpose for man has to be enveloped in our internal purpose.

We have heard the sad tales over and over again of those who have acquired what the world we look at calls material success, but the Bible poses the question: "What would it profit a man to gain the whole world and lose his soul."

This question is not to be looked at simply in light of what happens after we die because we make choices for our soul on a daily basis.

Even with this in mind, there are still those that believe that they can acquire enough materially to satisfy them for life.

Those that live with this mindset will be the ones for whom enough will never be enough.

They will spend all of their life's efforts getting more so that they can get more, but no matter how much they get, they will always be in want because the emptiness they need to fill can not be filled externally with the accumulation of things; the emptiness is in their souls.

This is only one side of the coin.

There will also be those who will seek to find satisfaction through other external measures.

We realize that sex, drugs and the consumption of alcohol are not the only sins in the Bible, but they are the most prevalent external measures that are usually delved into in an attempt to find fulfillment.

We spend our lives seeking to gain what the world has to offer to fulfill us, and some of these things will even add to our level of success. The problem is that, no matter how great our external successes are, when it comes to what we need internally, the vacuum is still empty if we have not properly responded to the first revelation.

What has been given to us to be lived out externally has to be wrapped in what is purposed for us internally because our purpose is not simply for our time. It is connected to eternity.

If we attempt to arrive at our ultimate purpose externally without what is necessary internally, we can only obtain an empty or perverse version of those gifts.

We can see this in a general sense in the whole of scripture and more specifically in the lives of men like Paul and Solomon.

Paul, whose name was Saul, before his conversion on the road to Damascus, was a gifted orator. He was well versed in the Law and a leader on the Sanhedrin Counsel.

In spite of these external exploits, Paul operated in his many gifts without what he needed internally. Paul's gifts became so perverted that he found himself leading bands of men on a mission to kill the servants of the very God who he thought he was serving.

Paul discovered, and became more than adequate in the exercise of his external gift, but it was merely a perversion of his purpose until he received what he needed internally.

In the case of Solomon, he was materially the most successful man ever known. His successes included the fulfilling of his external purpose to a degree that took him to the pinnacle of being when he was directed to build the Temple of God.

God was so pleased with this temple that He said that His "heart would be there perpetually."

If we didn't know any better, we would not believe that this is the same Solomon who penned the Book of Ecclesiastes.

Solomon was successful judicially, economically, and as a leader, even spiritually.

When we approach the subject of external success, Solomon would probably be the first to come to mind, but even with all of his success, it was Solomon who coined the phrase, "Vanity of vanities, all is vanity."

Solomon's quest for fulfilling his purpose externally, though seemingly complete, was void of satisfaction because he lost contact with his internal, eternal connection.

What is even more troubling about Solomon is that we see in him a man who had a connection and somewhere along the way he lost it.

What we see, when he lost his connection, is a man seeking to find satisfaction in the wealth of his surroundings.

If you were to read his story, you would find another recurring statement as he continually states, "There is no good thing under the sun."

We must understand that, just as it was for Solomon, it is for us. Even when we establish a connection with our intrinsic purpose, and accept Him as Lord of our lives, we still must continually maintain that connection, not in relation to salvation, but in order to fulfill our purpose.

If we do not, we can find ourselves in divine order one minute and lost in our own vain glory the next.

Therefore, if we are to properly respond to what God is revealing to us, we not only have to establish in our hearts the fact that there is more than one purpose being revealed, but we need to respond to both revelations.

If the question still remains, how can I know what God is revealing, or how can I know my purpose? My question is how can you not know it?

What I marvel at is the saved person who says, "I do not know what God would have for me to do?" If a lost person can discover what his gift is, how can a saved person not know his?

We approach it as if it is God's plan to keep it a secret.

We may not know everything that God has in store for us for our lifetimes, God's plan for our lives is one that is progressively revealed, but I do believe that God reveals to us what we need to know to fulfill our purpose for now.

Our problem is that we are waiting on God to just audibly tell us what to do.

Though this did happen on several occasions Biblically, and I believe continues to happen on some occasions now, I don't believe that this is how God reveals Himself as a matter of practice.

What we will more likely find is that God directs people to different places with different problems or shortcomings.

When He gets us in the place where he wants us to be, He reveals the problem to us.

These problems or shortcomings that He reveals to us are in line with the talents and gifts that God has given to us.

Have you ever wondered why a ministry can seem to be everything that you think it could possibly be and somebody shows up to reveal the places where that ministry is in need.

The reason for this is that God not only is always in the process of taking His church to the next level, but He also is in the process of using those that are willing to respond to the revelation.

If the body of Christ is to be what God would have it to be, locally and corporately, it will happen when God can find people to whom He can reveal problems that are willing to play their part in the process.

There are those who respond properly to the revelation.

What I am trying to say is that God leads us to the place where He wants us to be, He reveals to us what He would have us to do, but He does not make us do it.

There is a part we have to play, and that is responding to the revelation.

The reason why most ministries remain crippled and do not move to the level that God would have it to be is not because the church does not have what it needs. The reason why it remains in that condition is because we don't respond properly to the revelation.

You will find in most churches a ministry that is not listed in its bulletin.

I call it the critics' ministry.

The ministry usually consists of those whom God has allowed to see the problem in the church through the eyes of the gifts that He has placed in them, and instead of responding by exercising their gifts, they become critical of the church's shortcoming.

I hate to be the bearer of bad news, but for those of us who find ourselves in that boat, not only is criticism not a ministry; the critic does not even have a seat in the house of God.

Psalm 1 says: "Blessed is the man that walketh not in the counsel of the ungodly, nor standeth in the way of sinners, nor sitteth in the seat of the scornful (critic).

This principle holds true for our service in the church as well as it does for the work that God has for us outside of the church.

God allows us to see the world through eyes that He has only given to us. These eyes cause us to see the void that God wants us to not only fill but fulfill by utilizing the gifts that He has placed within us.

The question is not whether God is revealing to us what he would have us to do, the question is how are we handling what He has allowed us to see?

Therefore, if we are going to be what God would have us to be, we have to understand that our purpose is not simply external. We must understand that we are in a chain that links us to Adam in Genesis, and connects us to the end times of revelation.

Our purpose is not simply for our own personal benefit. It is a line that connects with eternity, and if we are going to fulfill it, ultimately we must respond properly to the revelations.

CHAPTER FIVE

RECEIVING THE INCREASE

As we established in our earlier chapters, God has given all of us gifts.

These gifts, which are part of the creation package, are given to us so that we would not only become a viable portion of society, but so that we could play a part in the improvement of the economy He places us in.

As we also discussed, these gifts are also given for the sake of our being of some significance to the Kingdom of God.

God does not give to us just so that we can improve upon our own personal situations, nor does He equip us just to make the world a better place, but He gives to us so that He can get glory through us as well.

It is now just as it was when Jesus stated in Matthew 5:16 that we are to "let (our) light so shine before men so that they might see (our) good works, and glorify the Father, which is in Heaven."

As beings, who are created in the Image and likeness of God, we understand that God is not in the business of hiding from us what he wants us to do. God is interested not only in the progress of society and His Kingdom, but He is ultimately interested in the salvation of man and equipping him so that he can disciple others.

Because this is the interest of God, it is in turn His interest that we come to the knowledge of what part we play in the process. Therefore, we must come to terms that God is revealing to us our purpose, and we have to respond properly to the revelation.

We understand that this revelation is progressive: where God reveals to us what He would have us do based upon the talents and abilities He has already placed inside of us.

In the progression of this revelation, we understand that in the giving to and revealing to us these gifts that we are created with comes the responsibility of improving upon these gifts.

I'm sure that this seems like a term that should not be in the same sentence with God when we speak in terms of improvement, but God places the responsibility on us to take what He has given to us and increase upon it.

So now that we have gone through the process of self-discovery, and have allowed God to put us in the position to fulfill our purpose, we must close by answering the question how do I make myself better or more fit for what God has called me to do.

We need to answer the question of how do I receive the increase.

To answer this, we will basically explore two areas for consideration.

The first thing that we need is application, or the need to apply ourselves. As I said earlier, God gives us gifts and abilities that He expects for us to improve upon. In order to do this, we have to apply ourselves.

This can be said for what God expects of us intrinsically and extrinsically.

Restoring the damage done to us intrinsically or spiritually, and becoming equipped for the role that we must play societally, requires us to apply ourselves to the study of our internal make up.

To put it simply, when it comes to spiritual matters, mere acceptance of God is enough for salvation, but it is not enough to accomplish everything that God wants us to do.

There is a healing, restoring and continual renewing process that must take place for us to fulfill the purpose that God has left for us to do.

This is why God left us with the entirety of His word to expand upon what He begins in the experience of salvation. In His word, God left us with the commandment in 2nd Timothy 2:15: "Study to show (ourselves) approved a workman unto God that needeth not be ashamed, rightly dividing the word of truth."

If we are to walk in the Spirit, live in the Spirit, and be moved by the Spirit, we have to grow in the Spirit.

Many of us do not accomplish the things that God would have us do because of past failure, or fear of the feeling that goes along with future disappointments.

This is part of the beauty of God's word because it shows us how all the great men of faith failed miserably and continually, but their failures decreased as their faith increased.

In order to increase our faith, we must become more acquainted with the will and the way of God through whom He revealed Himself to be in His word.

Faith is how the just make their living, and without faith, it is impossible to even please God.

Therefore, if we are to improve upon what God has begun in us spiritually, we have to allow Him to do it by audibly internalizing His word because, "Faith cometh by hearing and hearing by the word of God." (Romans 10:17)

We also have to improve upon the talents and gifts that we have been created with to operate in them properly extrinsically.

How we apply ourselves to this is a more difficult task to explain due the fact that there are so many different things that we can be gifted to do.

If we are gifted to work with our hands, this might call for us to improve upon it through some form of apprenticeship program.

Some might not look upon this as being a gift but some of the first men called to work for God were men gifted as master craftsmen, who were used in the building of the tabernacle.

If we are gifted to work in the technical fields, we might be required to improve upon it in training centers.

If we are gifted to be administrators in different fields of administration, it might call for us to apply ourselves in an institution of higher learning.

No matter when or where we find ourselves at the point of discovery, we must improve upon the gifts that God has given us to move to the level of a sense of fulfillment.

This improvement can be as simple as having some on-the-job training to as involved as eight years of schooling at a college or university.

Though the gifts, and what is necessary to accomplish them, are different, none can be considered as insignificant or not needed.

Our level of success and fulfillment in the eyesight of God is not so much in what we do, but in how we do what he has called us to do.

There is probably no worse feeling than spending a lifetime preparing ourselves for what we want to do only to find no peace or satisfaction in it because it is not what we are gifted to do. Equally as bad is the feeling that goes along with having been gifted to accomplish something and not fulfilling it because we have not applied ourselves at all.

Just as I stated in Chapter One, there will be some difficulties along the way. The devil has and still is placing things in our paths that call for us to make choices that alter our ultimate plan.

What Satan desires is that we will make enough bad choices to throw us totally off track from God's plan. He (the devil) wants us to view ourselves as having no worth or value, as total failures, but the good news is that God will take us, remold and reshape us, and put us back on the path He would have us follow.

This again is why we have to make the choice of responding to the first revelation.

You may have been gifted to be a doctor in God's original plan for your life, but made some choices that caused you not to reach that goal. In spite of that, God can take you and place you in other fields of healing and still cause you, to a great extent, to satisfy the burden that has been placed upon you.

What I am trying to say is that no matter where we find ourselves in the process today, God can take us and put us in a place where we can satisfy the burden that comes along with our gift, and at the same time satisfy Him.

It may not be where we were ultimately intended to be, but God will fill the void that we left by our bad choices.

So, if we are to receive what can be considered to be the increase, we have to apply ourselves to improve in the area of whatever it is that God has specifically gifted us to do.

The second thing that we must do to receive the increase is, while we are in the process of application, to be in continual rededication.

In order to fully realize what God has given us as potential, we have to do what seems to some degree backwards and in opposition to the first thing that we must do. In spite of how it sounds or how contrary it seems to be, while we are applying ourselves to improving on the gifts that God has given us, we must also be about the business of continually rededicating the gifts back to God.

What I am suggesting is that in order to get what God wants to give us out of the gifts He has given us, we have to unceasingly dedicate them back to Him.

Just like Hannah did with Samuel, we have to do with our gifts. We have to not only remember where they came from, but willingly give them back to Him so that He can cause us to reach our fullest in them.

As backwards as it may sound, it just makes good common sense.

If it is God that creates it in us, it is God that knows how to get the best out of them from us.

This is a part of the basic cycle that God has established for all of life.

God has said in his word, "Give and I'll give it back to you, good measure, pressed down, shaken together and running over shall men give into your bosom." This statement is made with the knowledge that what He is asking us to give is a portion what He has given to us.

It is the principle of reaping and sowing. Whatever I am willing to sow I understand that I can reap a harvest that much greater, and that there is no harvest if I choose not to sow.

If we want, not just an increase but "the increase", we have got to rededicate our gifts to Him.

We have these gifts only because He has given them to us, and just as He stated in the parable of the talents, He expects some return on His investment.

God deserves all the glory for them, He deserves all the glory from them, and He should get to glory in them. This will only happen when we give them back to Him.

Our gifts are not truly alive until we give them back to God and allow him to do through the Spirit the same thing that he did when He created man.

God wants to breathe on them and give them life so that we, through them can have life more abundantly.

I know that these are verses of scripture that are usually associated with prosperity, but what I am speaking of is a different level of prosperity.

This is prosperity where I take what God has given to me as my purpose for being, and I give it back to Him. In return He gives me an increase.

This increase is not subject to situation or circumstance.

It is the nature of the cycle.

If God is pleased with me, then I will be blessed through Him.

With this type or level of prosperity it does not matter where I am, or what I've got, I will be content, because my contentment will come from Him.

It is true that, when we apply ourselves, that the level to which we give ourselves to this application will greatly determine our level of material prosperity, but material prosperity will by no means determine our level of satisfaction. This will only come through the level in which we dedicate our gifts to God.

When we come to grips with this, we will no longer seek to find our self-worth in what we do.

The idea of "who I am" is determined by "what I do" is carnal, and worldly, and a trick used by the devil. Part of Satan's job is not only to confuse us about who we are, but also about what we are supposed to do.

This is what he did with Adam when he convinced him that subduing the earth was not significant enough a task. He convinced Adam that who he was, and what God wanted him to do was nothing when compared to the proposition of being as God.

This is why we need to be totally sold on the idea of continual rededication because it allows us to no longer equate our self-worth with what we do.

When we do this, who we are and how we see ourselves, will no longer be through the eyes of our vocation. Our self-worth will be based on discovering the part we play in this eternal process, and how we use that part to improve upon society and carry out the cause of Christ.

What adds even more to the level of fulfillment is the fact that no matter where we find ourselves right now, God wants to meet us in that place of the process.

God desires to take all of our faults, failures and what we consider to be misfortune and remove the bitter taste that they leave in our soul and replace it with the sweet taste of contentment.

This is a level of prosperity that takes us beyond our wallets and our pocketbooks.

This type of prosperity is not determined by the size of bank accounts or our financial portfolios.

This is a prosperity that will allow us to find the peace that passes all understanding because we put ourselves in the position to find favor with God and man.

When we seek our increase through giving our gifts back to God, when it's all said and done, we can look to Heaven and with confidence repeat the mantra of Paul when he said, "I fought the good fight, I have finished my course, I have kept the faith. Henceforth is laid up for me a crown of righteousness..."

Paul was able to say this in spite of all of his past faults and failures. He was able to say this because, when He was on the wrong road in life, he met God. And when he met God on that wrong road, he asked the right question.

After Paul discovered what God wanted him to do, he went through the process of application and rededication.

Paul was in pain and imprisoned, but he was given grace that was sufficient and strength that was perfect in his weakness.

When we live out the purpose that God has designed for us, we can experience a small taste of Heaven while we live here in earth, but we can only enjoy this when we let His will be done in earth as it is in Heaven.

When we do this, and can honestly say that we have finished our course in return we can expect the ultimate increase when God responds, "Well done my good and faithful servant. Thou has been faithful over a few things, I will make you ruler over many. Enter into the joy of the Lord."

ABOUT THE AUTHOR

Charles Thomas, Jr. is an Associate Minister at the Zion Hope Missionary Baptist Church in Detroit, MI. Born the 4th of 10 children, he grew up in an environment where money was at a premium.

This along with the gang violence that was the order of the day moved him to make decisions that caused others to count him out.

Traumatic experiences that were a result of his decisions led him down a road of self-destruction, but God and the revelation of His purpose opened the door to a more excellent way.

"What Is My Purpose" answer the question of how you can experience the fulfillment that comes along with being who you were created to be.

www.ingramcontent.com/pod-product-compliance
Ingram Content Group UK Ltd.
Pitfield, Milton Keynes, MK11 3LW, UK
UKHW040016200726
13854UKWH00001B/234

9 780759 608979